Mozart: The Piano Concerti

BLACK DOG MUSIC LIBRARY

Mozart: The Piano Concerti

Piano Concerto No. 20 in D minor, *K. 466*

Piano Concerto No. 21 in C, *K. 467,* (*Elvira Madigan)*

TEXT BY DAVID FOIL

BLACK DOG & LEVENTHAL PUBLISHERS
NEW YORK

Published by
Black Dog & Leventhal Publishers Inc.
151 West 19th Street
New York, NY 10011

Distributed by
Workman Publishing Company
708 Broadway
New York, NY 10003

Designed by Martin Lubin and Allison Russo

Special thanks to Judith Dupré

Book manufactured in Hong Kong

ISBN: 1-884822-38-X

*N*owhere is the vast genius and magnificence of Wolfgang Amadeus Mozart better expressed than in his great piano concerti. His form and symmetry, his passion and his beauty, his richness and his power are all exemplified here. The Piano Concerto in D minor, K. 466 and the Piano Concerto in C, K. 467 (*Elvira Madigan*) are incomparable, flawless works. In this volume you will be able to read and learn about Mozart, the man and the composer; you will better understand the importance, the meaning, the message, and the structure of his great orchestral works; and you can enjoy and listen to the music as you read.

Play the compact disc included on the inside front cover of this book and follow along with the musical commentary and analysis. Please note that the times of the relevant musical passages are noted for your convenience.

Enjoy this book and enjoy the music.

Wolfgang Amadeus Mozart

Leopold Mozart arrived in Vienna early in the afternoon of February 10, 1785, to find his twenty-nine-year-old son Wolfgang Amadeus racing to finish the orchestral parts for a new piano concerto that would premiere that evening. The Lenten season was under way in Vienna, and public concerts were more likely than ever to draw a fashionable crowd starved for diversion. As he had the year before, the young composer had assembled an orchestra and found an audience-friendly venue—in this case, a hotel-restaurant with a ballroom called the Mehlgrube—for a subscription series of concerts that would feature his music. This daring enterprise was virtually without precedent. Such concerts were rare outside churches and aristocratic salons, and no composer in Vienna had been so boldly ambitious about creating an audience for his music.

No one who knew Wolfgang Amadeus Mozart could have doubted his ability to prevail in such a situation. He was determined to have a new concerto for the first program, even though only two months previously he had completed a perfectly beautiful piano concerto, the delightful F major. In a letter to his daughter Nannerl dated February 16, Leopold Mozart described in matter-of-fact terms the activities surrounding the concert: "We went to his first subscription concert that evening, where a great many from the aristocracy

Wolfgang Amadeus Mozart as a child.

were in the audience. The concert was magnificent and the orchestra splendid. In addition to the symphonies, a female singer from the Italian theater sang two arias. Then we heard the new and superb concerto by Wolfgang that was still being copied out when we arrived, and your brother had no time even to play through the Rondo, since he had to supervise the copying."

This concerto, in D minor and generally numbered the twentieth of his twenty-seven concertos for piano and orchestra, is one of Mozart's supreme masterpieces. Even when his piano concertos fell out of favor during the nineteenth century, this one continued to be played. A work of daring intensity and violent drama, the D minor concerto seems to bristle at the limitations of the Classical style, anticipating the *Sturm und Drang* of the burgeoning Romantic age. Not surprisingly, Ludwig van Beethoven, never Mozart's biggest fan, was one of the concerto's most compelling advocates. Some commentators have called it the most "Beethovenian" of Mozart's concertos, which, while intended as a compliment, diminishes the startling originality of the work.

If the experience of Mozart's music teaches us anything, though, it is to surrender our expectations. A member of the smart audience at the Mehlgrube might have wondered if the composer was reconsidering his style or, at the very least, entering a "dark" period. After all, Mozart wrote very little music in the key of D minor, and frequently turned to it in his operas when he wanted to depict conflict, violence, and a vengeful mood.

In fact, Mozart was enjoying one of his more successful years. Less than a month after the unveiling of the D minor, he completed yet another piano concerto, performed this time in a concert at Vienna's Burgtheater. The new concerto, in C major and generally numbered the twenty-first, was a stunning about-face; it is a work of dazzling charm and beauty that seems to enshrine the nobility, equilibrium, and lucid elegance of Classical music at its most refined. Nearly two centuries after its premiere, the Swedish filmmaker Bo Widerberg used a recording of the C major's slow movement on the soundtrack of his 1967 film *Elvira Madigan*, a visually arresting love story that enjoyed great international success. The film's popularity made recordings of Mozart's C major concerto instant best-sellers. The music became so strongly identified with Widerberg's hypnotic imagery that it is still referred to as the *Elvira Madigan* concerto.

Vienna's Burgtheater

The piano concertos Mozart wrote for his Viennese concerts in the 1780s are reckoned among his finest achievements in instrumental music. They combine his mastery of form with visionary ideas of what the concerto could be. Taking what was a quaint, diverting, and occasionally provocative showcase for the keyboard artist, Mozart transformed the concerto into a serious, truly symphonic medium in which the soloist and the orchestra became responsive and eloquent partners.

His Life

The facts of Wolfgang Amadeus Mozart's life and art are so unusual that it is easy to think of him as a kind of glorious freak, a divine creature, or a mere medium for the heavenly inspiration that flowed through him with so little apparent effort. Peter Shaffer's entertaining, popular play *Amadeus* and its award-winning film adaptation enhance this image. So does the reverence musicians have accorded Mozart over the years, which frequently borders on sentimentality. "Beethoven is always storming Heaven," the conductor Josef Krips reportedly once told an orchestra, "but Mozart! Mozart *lives* there!" Today Mozart's memory is enshrined as well in his hometown of Salzburg, where his name appears on everything from concert halls to candy. Ironically, he detested his life there and fled at the first opportunity in 1781, after which neither the town nor its citizens had much use for him until many years after his death, when the association with him became profitable.

Mozart's genius *was* miraculous in its breadth and depth, but it must be said that he more than fulfilled its promise, in a sometimes poisonous atmosphere and under trying personal circumstances. However, he was hardly a saint. By all accounts he could be a vexing, even obnoxious guest at social gatherings, and the endless delight his letters reveal in sharing jokes about flatulence does not quite square with the image of a composer of sublime music. Like Johann Sebastian Bach or any artist with a profoundly spiritual side, Mozart was a passionate man. He played hard and worked hard, as the circumstances surrounding the premiere of the D minor concerto indicate. If music poured out of him in perfect order, he still doggedly saw to it that the parts were correct, the details observed, and the performance prepared.

Painting of Mozart in the collection of the Bologna Conservatory.

Leopold Mozart's account of that 1785 concert noted the quality of the performance—a performance in which a pickup orchestra virtually sight-read the most demanding and subtly expressive piano concerto anyone had ever written. Mozart conducted from the keyboard—he had not even had time to play through the last movement— and the technical skill and razor-sharp reflexes that galvanized and propelled this historic performance were a wonder.

Mozart was born in Salzburg on January 27, 1756, and baptized the following day as Joannes Chrysostomus

Wolfgangus Theophilus Mozart. The first two names refer to the fact that January 27 is the feast day of St. John Chrysostom; the third was his grandfather's name, and the fourth was his godfather's. Where is *Amadeus*? *Theophilus* comes from the Greek for "beloved of God," but Mozart apparently preferred the Latin form, *Amadeus*, and sometimes the German form, *Gottlieb*.

Six children were born to Leopold and Anna Maria Pertl Mozart, of whom Wolfgang was the fourth. Only he and his sister Maria Anna—born in 1751 and known affectionately as Nannerl—survived infancy. He inherited no great musical legacy. Mozart's ancestors included a number of craftsmen, artisans, and public servants, and his father turned to music only after studying philosophy and law. Leopold Mozart took a job as violinist in the service of Salzburg's prince-archbishop and, a few years after Wolfgang's birth, rose to the rank of deputy *Kapellmeister* (musical director).

Mozart and his sister Nannerl at the keyboard with their father.

Mozart's first composition, 1761

Whatever the origins of Wolfgang Amadeus Mozart's musical gifts, they announced themselves early and decisively. There is evidence that he was playing pieces from Nannerl's music book when he was four, and his father recorded his first compositions—a simple andante and allegro—the following year. That year, 1761, Mozart made his first public appearance in Salzburg, which inspired Leopold to take the boy and his sister on the road. By the end of 1762, they had been to Munich and had even played in Vienna for the Empress Maria Theresa. Leopold Mozart was a true stage father, taking full advantage of his son's emerging gifts. Their concerts were more sideshows than recitals—the young Mozart played blindfolded or with a cloth over the keys, improvised new material in any style requested, perfectly sight-read music he had never seen, and displayed his remarkable ear by identifying any note played for him.

These concerts continued with few breaks for the next decade, in long and arduous tours across Europe that became more substantial as both Mozart and the dimensions of his genius grew. It was a fabulous life in many ways. The crowned heads of Europe acclaimed the boy, lavishing gifts and trinkets on him and his family. Experts devised ever more demanding tests for his musical skills, which he always passed with breathtaking ease.

While the family visited Rome during Holy Week in 1770, one of the great Mozart legends was born. After hearing the Sistine Chapel choir sing the *Miserere* of Gregorio Allegri—a beautiful and complex choral work that only this choir performed—Mozart reportedly sat down and wrote out the entire piece from memory. Even if, as some have suggested, Mozart had had the opportunity to look at the manuscript, the concentration this stunt required was staggering. Later stories would corroborate his mental powers. Friends would remember Mozart composing while he drank and chatted at parties, and his autograph scores are famous for their pristine accuracy.

Inevitably, the vogue for Mozart the Wunderkind faded. The angelic child developed into an odd-looking, awkward young man, and his bag of

Mozart's home in Salzburg.

musical tricks lost its appeal. But Mozart had been composing steadily throughout his childhood and adolescence. A month before his fifteenth birthday, on December 26, 1770, *Mitridate, rè di Ponto*, his full-scale opera in the elevated *opera seria* style of the day, had its premiere at Milan's Regio Ducal Teatro. By the time he had reached physical maturity, he was a veteran composer with a large body of work.

Despite his international fame, Mozart was unsuccessful in finding a post as court composer. Late in 1771, the Austrian Empress Maria

Salzburg today.

Theresa, an early fan, wrote to her son, the Archduke Ferdinand, advising him against hiring the fifteen-year-old composer because the Mozart family's "going about the world like beggars" would embarrass the royal household.

Ultimately Mozart returned to Salzburg, where, like his father, he went into the service of the city's prince-archbishop, now a rigid, controlling man named Hieronymus, Count Colloredo. Colloredo had a low regard for music as a purely aesthetic medium and was strict and inflexible when it came to church music. His reforms reduced the amount of music played in church and at court, and he closed Salzburg's theaters. Mozart chafed at these restrictions and even more so at the way Colloredo inhibited his personal advancement. The archbishop took offense at Mozart's ambition and frequently denied his requests to travel, even when he had a commission elsewhere. Mozart quit in 1777 and traveled to the musical centers of Mannheim and Paris in the company of his mother (who died during the journey), only to return to Salzburg, miserable once again in the archbishop's service, this time as an organist.

A scene from Mozart's opera Idomeneo *at Salzburg's historic Felsenreitschule.*

The one bright spot was a long-hoped-for commission from Munich to write an opera, which resulted in *Idomeneo*. The premiere, two days after Mozart's twenty-fifth birthday, was a success, and a lengthy stay in Munich seemed to restore his confidence in finding a stable life outside Salzburg. A short while later Colloredo ordered him to Vienna as part of the archbishop's household for the celebrations surrounding the accession of a new emperor, Joseph II. There Mozart was subjected to small but numerous humiliations: At dinner, for instance, he was seated among the household servants. So petty was the archbishop that he refused Mozart's request to perform

Title page of The Abduction from the Seraglio.

in concerts in Vienna. The final break came in the spring of 1781, after an ugly encounter with the archbishop, who apparently shocked even Mozart with the vehemence of his anger. At last, though, the composer would be free to pursue his career in Vienna.

While in Vienna, Mozart left the archbishop's household and moved in with a family named Weber whom he had come to know some years earlier during a visit to Mannheim. While in Mannheim in 1777, he had become infatuated with Aloysia Weber, the family's sixteen-year-old daughter, a fine soprano whom he had considered taking to Italy and making into a prima donna. (Leopold had been enraged by this plan.) Four years later Aloysia had married, and so—while he apparently never lost his affection for her—Mozart turned his attentions to her younger sister Constanze. The courtship continued into 1782, while the composer taught private students and worked on a *Singspiel* titled *Die Entführung aus dem Serail* (*The Abduction from the Seraglio*).

Mozart's wife Constanze

Singspiel, a German term meaning "song play," is the equivalent of the Italian *dramma per musica*. It was not unlike an operetta or a musical, and the language of its spoken dialogue and sung text was German, the vernacular tongue in Vienna. Though now grouped together, *Singspiel* and opera (which was always sung in Italian) were different creatures in Mozart's day. Unlike *Singspiel*, opera was usually entirely sung, even in the recitatives, the conversational patches that connect arias and ensembles. Mozart wrote a second, more famous *Singspiel, Die Zauberflöte (The Magic Flute)*, in 1791.

As Mozart worked toward a stage premiere for *Die Entführung aus dem Serail*, he decided to marry Constanze Weber, whose mother was apparently scheming along these same lines. With the Emperor Joseph II in attendance, the *Singspiel's* premiere seems to have been a success. It inspired the famous, perhaps apocryphal, exchange between sovereign and composer. "Too many notes," Joseph II is reputed to have said, to which Mozart replied, "Exactly the right number, Your Majesty." This important debut, the need to produce an income, and his impending marriage did not stifle Mozart's creativity. He wrote a set of piano concertos and the first of his string quartets during this period.

Emperor Joseph II

Mozart's marriage to Constanze took place early in August 1782; Leopold gave his consent under protest and only at the last minute. With so many people who had vested interests observing the marriage, particularly Leopold, it is small wonder that the union has been made to seem pitiable.

The sumptuous Rococo Room in Vienna's Schönbrun Palace, where Mozart performed.

Constanze was apparently a sensible, kind, and loving woman and utterly devoted to her husband, even if she was not a witty sophisticate or Mozart's intellectual equal. Unfortunately, instead of providing stability, marriage seemed to magnify Mozart's extravagance and procrastination. In 1783 the Mozarts had their first child, a son who only lived a few weeks. Five children followed, though only two survived infancy: Karl Thomas Mozart and Franz Xaver Wolfgang Mozart, both of whom lived well into the mid-nineteenth century.

Late in 1783 the couple journeyed to Salzburg, with fear and loathing. Mozart worried that the archbishop might have him arrested and fretted even more about the reception they would receive from his father. Leopold Mozart, ever the jealous and ambitious parent, was appalled by his daughter-in-law and did little to conceal his contempt. The Mozarts' return to Vienna included a stop in Linz, where the composer, who had no music with him, satisfied his hosts with a legendary bit of face-saving. At what he called "breakneck speed," he dashed off the C major symphony that now bears the number 36 and the title *Linz*. Upon his return Mozart became interested in the Freemasons and joined the Masonic order in 1784.

Mozart's creative output in the early 1780s seems to have justified his insistence on moving to Vienna. New music flowed from his pen at an amazing rate. In 1784 he began to exploit the Lenten season concerts in order to increase awareness of his work and add to his income. His financial problems continued, however. He had hoped for the stability of a court appointment, but none was forthcoming. His income, though not insignificant, was unpredictable. The Mozarts were always in debt and hard pressed to pay for their lavish lifestyle. They were plagued as well by intrigue and gossip, one of the more virulent aspects of the Viennese musical scene. Mozart's rivals did scheme against him, among them Antonio Salieri, though there is little evidence to suggest the psychotic vendetta sketched in Shaffer's *Amadeus*. But such scheming certainly would have worked against Mozart's efforts to win a coveted court position.

As with most composers at the time, opera was of paramount importance to Mozart. Most of his operas are either *opera seria* (serious opera)—formal, elevated works, often on mythological subjects, with brilliant vocal writing (these include *Mitridate*, *Idomeneo*, and *La Clemenza di Tito*)—or *opera buffa* (comic opera), such as *Le nozze di Figaro. Don Giovanni* carries a distinctively different label of *dramma giocoso*, or comic drama.

In 1783 an abandoned comic opera project brought him into contact with a brilliant writer named Lorenzo da Ponte. Their first real collaboration came in 1785–86, in an adaptation of Beaumarchais's controversial comedy *Le mariage de Figaro*. Composition of the opera, written in Italian, was apparently begun in the fall of 1785; the successful premiere, in Vienna,

Leontyne Price as Donna Anna in Mozart's operatic masterpiece Don Giovanni.

came the following spring, despite intrigue surrounding the project to which Salieri may have been a party.

The opera's popularity led to a premiere in Prague, where Mozart found a receptive audience (for which he wrote a symphony, his thirty-eighth, which bears the title *Prague*) and an impresario who commissioned a new opera. The new work was *Don Giovanni*, arguably Mozart's operatic master-piece, and another da Ponte collaboration. It had a tumultuous Prague premiere in the fall of 1787. Viennese audiences were cooler, though, and their indif-ferent reception of *Don Giovanni* said much about the regard they had for Mozart and his music.

The composer's financial problems grew steadily worse. He traveled as far as Frankfurt and London in search of commissions, which did not cover his debts. Mozart was churning out one masterpiece after another, in the vain hope that one of them would pay off handsomely. In a single six-week period in the summer of 1788, a year that was especially productive if not profitable, Mozart composed his last three symphonies—a stupendous achievement. Nothing, however, seemed to bring him lasting success—not the symphonies, not another da Ponte opera (the sublime comedy *Così fan tutte*), not the later, even more masterful piano concertos, not the chamber music that had become his favorite new medium.

The intensity with which Mozart lived and worked took a terrible toll on his health. Late in the summer of 1791, he fell ill while in Prague for the premiere of his last stage work, the opera seria *La Clemenza di Tito*. Still ailing, he returned to Vienna and worked on a commissioned setting of the *Requiem Mass* which he would not finish. The last works he completed were his Clarinet Concerto and a Masonic cantata, the premiere of which he conducted on November 18 at his Masonic lodge. Mozart never fully recovered from what is now thought to have been rheumatic inflammatory fever, and he died early on the morning of December 5, 1791, at the age of thirty-five.

Mozart's Influence

In the same letter that described the 1785 premiere of the D minor piano concerto, Leopold Mozart wrote about attending another performance of some of the six string quartets Wolfgang had written and dedicated to Haydn. Leopold relayed to Nannerl that Haydn, honored and delighted by the music, said to him, "I tell you, calling God to witness and speaking as a man of honor, that your son is the greatest composer I know, either personally or by repute! He has taste, and, in addition, the most complete understanding of composition."

Haydn's opinion of Mozart was well known; the admiration between the two was warm and mutual. While Mozart had many admirers in his own day, his influence was not as widely acknowledged as that of, say, Christoph Willibald Gluck, who was famous for his reform of opera. Beethoven, who had impressed Mozart as a young virtuoso and even played Mozart's D minor concerto, made it a point to tell people that he held neither Mozart nor Haydn (who was his teacher for a brief, unhappy time) in as high regard as he did Antonio Salieri, whom legend has cast as Mozart's *bête noire*. Salieri, in fact, was one of the most successful teachers in the history of music, in terms of results—Beethoven,

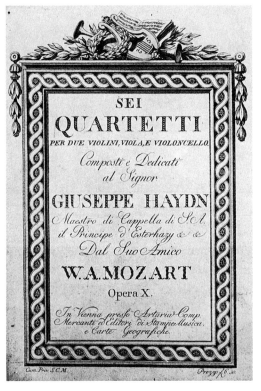

Schubert and Liszt were among his students. Certainly Salieri was more successful in his day than Mozart, whom he outlived by thirty-four years.

Mozart's influence is keenly felt in the music of Felix Mendelssohn, who in turn became a paragon for many composers of the Romantic era. Mendelssohn synthesized some of the finest qualities of Mozart's music in an original Romantic style. Like Mozart, he was an astonishing prodigy who began composing as a child and died before reaching the age of forty.

Title page of Sei quartetti, *1785, dedicated to Joseph Haydn.*

Ant. Salieri
nat. a Legnago 19 Ag.
1750

Fr. Rehberg as viv del
Vienna 6 febr. 1821

Antonio Salieri

Antonio Salieri

Frédéric Chopin had little or no use for most Romantic music; his twin gods were Bach and Mozart.

Though Mozart was held in high regard and his music never left the repertoire, Beethoven and Mendelssohn were the models for nineteenth-century composers, followed by Liszt and the warring factions of Brahms and Wagner. The modern revival of Mozart probably dates from Gustav Mahler's famous productions at the turn of the twentieth century of *Don Giovanni* and *Le nozze di Figaro* at the Court Opera in Vienna. Throughout this century, interest in Mozart has only increased. By 1991, when the 200th anniversary of Mozart's death was commemorated, every note of music he was known to have written had been analyzed, performed, and recorded many times over. Today a virtual industry of Mozart exists. At long last, his very name is "good box office" and—for individual soloists and singers, orchestras, opera companies, and recording companies—a guaranteed moneymaker. The irony is rich.

The Concerto

The concerto had existed as a musical form for more than a century before Mozart's time. At first the term described a composition for voice that was supported by an instrumental accompaniment—literally, "in concert"—to distinguish it from a composition that was sung unaccompanied, or *a cappella*. A form of the concerto that was completely instrumental emerged during the Baroque era and described a work in which different bodies of instruments played alternately and in contrast. The Italian *concerto grosso*, featuring a smaller body of instruments playing with the full orchestra,

began to take a definitive shape in the late seventeenth century and comprised three movements in a fast-slow-fast arrangement. Johann Sebastian Bach retained the Italian model but began spotlighting a single solo instrument instead of the *concerto grosso's* ensemble. George Frideric Handel made further innovations with his popularization of the cadenza, a passage near the end of a movement that allows the soloist to improvise. But it was Mozart who—without

Gustav Mahler

disturbing its Classical structure—transformed the concerto into a definitive symphonic musical medium.

Twenty-seven of Mozart's works bear the designation "piano concerto" in the 1964 Köchel catalog of Mozart's complete works. The first four were simply orchestrated and refashioned from keyboard works by other composers (C.P.E. Bach among them). The first wholly original Mozart piano concerto is the fifth one, in D major, written in 1773.

Mozart returned to the format at regular intervals throughout his career, as it allowed him to display his facility as a performer. Mozart's catalog includes five violin concertos—all first-rate and written in the last six months of 1775—and a half-dozen more concertos for strings. In addition, he wrote more than a dozen concertos for flute, oboe, bassoon, trumpet, horn, and clarinet; works for these instruments in combination; and a popular concerto for flute and harp. The finest of his piano concertos (generally the last seven, which include the two heard here) are as remarkable as anything he wrote.

Mozart transformed the concerto by integrating into it the plan known as sonata form. Sonata form suggests the layout of the opening movement of a sonata—a string quartet, a concerto, or a symphony—and it also suggests the relationship of musical keys to be used within the movement. The rules of sonata form frequently change, especially in Romantic music, but the standard design generally holds in Classical works. In the opening section, called the exposition, two themes are presented, usually contrasting both in character and in their keys. The first theme is sometimes repeated before a modulation leads into the second major section, called the development. Here material from the exposition is elaborated upon—sometimes at length and with great complexity—as it works its way back into the original key.

Once that is achieved, the first theme is repeated, signaling the beginning of the recapitulation, in which the music of the exposition is heard again but in an altered form. It is often followed by the coda, a section that usually contains the cadenza and carries the entire movement to its conclusion.

At the time, cadenzas were essential features of any piano concerto because they gave the soloist the opportunity to display his improvisational ability. Soloists used these moments to elaborate on the composer's thematic material in a crowd-pleasing display of virtuosity. Sometimes these cadenzas

Mozart was buried in 1791 in an unmarked grave in St. Mark's Cemetery in Vienna. Aficionados of his music erected this marker at his grave in 1859.

were notated, though Mozart apparently did not set down his own cadenzas for the D minor concerto (as he did occasionally for others); fortunately, we have Beethoven's. In the Romantic age, as the popularity of improvisation began to fade, the cadenza was usually written out by the composer, thus ensuring the detailed unity of expression, texture, and atmosphere that is an essential feature of Romantic music.

To appreciate and enjoy Mozart's concertos, it is not necessary to know and understand sonata form. As the craft that supports the art, sonata form is most effective when the listener is not even aware of it. Where Mozart is concerned, the inspiration and quality of his work are so extraordinary that we do not have to think about how he gets from A to Z—we want to follow him anyway. What sonata form offers the composer is a method for organizing his musical ideas and creating a tension that can be resolved in an interesting and compelling manner.

What about the other two movements?

The slow movements provide a period of calm after the domineering action of the first movements. Sometimes they are structured, sometimes not. Each of the concertos we are exploring concludes, in the Classical style, with a rondo. By Mozart's time the rondo had developed into a structure not unlike sonata form. It was based on a series of three episodes called couplets (a term borrowed from French medieval poetry), and bound by a reiterated musical subject called the refrain. The first and third couplets often function like the exposition and recapitulation in sonata form, and the second often resembles the development. Mozart's rondos seem to defy the limitations of structure. They are dazzling, irresistible creations, concluding his concertos with a brilliance that seems like a force of nature.

Mozart's Instruments

For what kind of keyboard instrument did Mozart write these concertos? In Mozart's lifetime, the harpsichord had given way to the piano, and his mature keyboard works almost certainly were written for the piano, though not, obviously, the kind of instrument Annie Fischer plays on these recordings. The evolution of the piano into the brilliant, virtuosic concert instrument we know today continued throughout most of the nineteenth century.

The pianos Mozart knew and played had a smaller, more limited keyboard than the modern piano, and whose tone tended to be warmer and less biting and percussive. While earlier pianos had a more restricted dynamic range, Mozart exploited the warmth of their sound and their potential for creating a flowing, songlike musical line. Listen to his orchestrations in these concertos: They have a mellowness and a fluency that had never before existed in concerto scoring. Liberated from the brilliant but pinched, one-dimensional sound of the harpsichord, he turns the keyboard concerto—once merely a showcase—into a new and richly expressive medium.

Köchel Numbering

The "K." that appears in the title of every Mozart composition refers to the work's catalog number. In the nineteenth century, with an eye toward

A Grand Pianoforte by Jacob Bertsche, Vienna, circa 1815.

posterity, composers began cataloging their own compositions. In Mozart's day, however, this was unheard of, and that is why his music, along with that of Bach and Haydn, has unique catalog numbering.

The "K." in Mozart's titles stands for "Köchel," referring to Ludwig von Köchel (1800–1877), the Austrian botanist and mineralogist whose abiding love for Mozart led him to create the first definitive catalog of his music. Köchel set about his task with the probity and patience of a scientist, finally publishing in 1862 the massive *Chronologisch-thematisches Verzeichnis sämtlicher Tonwerke von Wolfgang Amade Mozarts* (*Chronological Thematic Catalog of the Musical Works of Wolfgang Amadeus Mozart*). A second edition appeared in 1905, and the catalog was extensively revised and updated in 1937 by the musicologist Alfred Einstein. Other updates have been made as previously unknown material and historical information have come to light. However, Köchel's numbering remains the standard.

CONCERTO NO. 20 IN D MINOR, *K. 466*

THE FIRST MOVEMENT *Allegro* (*Quickly*). Crisis looms immediately: Softly but ominously, the same note pulses in a syncopated rhythm, with a grim flourish of three rising notes that is repeated to drive home the sense of foreboding. The first fifteen measures (⬚1 0:01-0:30) sketch the character of the whole movement, which is streaked with conflict and violence—moods Mozart was more likely to explore in his operas (*Don Giovanni* never seems far away here) than in his piano concertos. Against the muttering of the opening figures, a melody emerges (⬚1 0:31) that adds to the tension, rising (with woodwinds joining the strings) and then falling away until a sudden fortissimo shifts the mood violently (⬚1 0:52). The orchestra is unleashed, with glints of brass, to repeat the opening with an energy that, instead of brute force, suggests passion.

The uproar yields to the second subject (1 1:01), announced by the flute and oboes. It is a dialogue of short phrases that gives way to a wistful series of sighs in the violins, which returns the music (1 1:12) to the opening key of D minor. The air of conflict is back, with a heightened intensity, until a sudden drop to *piano* (meaning softly) (1 2:03) brings on the concluding subject, a nervous but vulnerable statement that prepares us for the arrival of the soloist. It is an extraordinary moment (1 2:21), highly original and perfectly judged, in which the piano freely sings a theme rich in pathos and yearning, like a character in an operatic aria. As the theme drifts off, the movement's throbbing opening bars return (1 2:47) with the soloist adding to the tension and transforming the restatement that follows. A change of key to F major (1 3:28) alters the mood, now galvanized by a powerful and bravura passage (1 4:20) for the soloist that deepens the drama. The orchestra returns with even greater strength (1 5:12), bringing the exposition to a memorable close that is imbued with anticipation.

The development section (1 5:44) brings the soloist and the orchestra into a closer dialogue. The soloist twice tries to make a clearer statement of its original theme, but each time the movement's opening returns. Before abandoning all hope, the soloist tries once more (1 6:10), calling down a new fierceness that infects the orchestra (1 10:31) and eventually returns to the D minor opening, signaling the recapitulation. The atmosphere now is not one of shock but of inevitability: The conflict will continue with little hope of relief or victory.

We arrive at the cadenza (1 10:51), which in this recording is Beethoven's (Mozart apparently did not write down his own cadenzas for this concerto), a moment for the soloist to meditate upon and make some sense of what has transpired. The orchestra returns (⏹1⏹ 12:53) to bring the movement to a close. With the fires still burning, the final subject describes heartrending sorrow and isolation, and ends not with a bang, but a whimper.

THE SECOND MOVEMENT *Romanza* (*Romance*). Then, sheer bliss. Though Mozart called this movement a *romanza*, it follows the plan of a rondo. Unaccompanied, the piano announces the main subject of the refrain, a melody of such easy, witty grace and limpid beauty that it stands out even by Mozartean standards. The orchestra picks it up (⏹2⏹0:27), and the soloist offers a secondary theme (⏹2⏹0:52) that leads back to the opening. The first couplet (⏹2⏹2:06) extends the mood and returns to the refrain (⏹2⏹3:43), before the second couplet (⏹2⏹4:35) shatters this dreamy atmosphere. Given the heavenly opening theme, the spasm of violence introduced by the second couplet is shocking. A long transitional section (⏹2⏹5:20) follows its two themes, leading us at long last back to the calm of the opening (⏹2⏹7:23), a calm that now has a more meaningful presence and that brings this movement to a close.

THE THIRD MOVEMENT *Rondo: Allegro assai* (*Very quickly*). With the idyll (however troubled) ended, we are once again amid the action. The soloist announces the primary theme of the refrain and then vanishes for a lengthy and stunning development in the orchestra (⏹3⏹0:11). The piano returns to announce the first couplet with a palpitating subject (⏹3⏹0:55) that gives way to the music of the refrain and a restless pursuit of calm that finally arrives in a new theme (⏹3⏹1:38), a beautiful Mozartean inspiration. The soloist keeps moving and eventually loses the thread of reassurance. The second couplet (⏹3⏹3:00), a vivid dialogue between piano and orchestra, acts as a development section. Instead of returning to the refrain, as sonata-rondo form would suggest, Mozart plunges (③4:01) directly into the third couplet, the recapitulation, once again in the signature key of D minor. The atmosphere is clouded but full of expectation, and the return of the orchestra leads to the cadenza (③5:09), also by Beethoven. The orchestra does not reenter afterward in a conventional manner; the soloist refers to the refrain (③ 6:16), then shatters the momentum, leaving us suspended in silence for a second. The horns enter (③6:24), followed by the basses and a curiously merry tune in the oboes (③6:25) that the soloist assumes. The frenzy that follows, bringing the movement and the entire concerto to a close, offers some relief from the tempest we have experienced. Primarily, though, the close is what one commentator called a "triumph over sorrow by distraction," a response to conflict so typical of the twentieth century that it reminds us how timeless Mozart's genius can be.

CONCERTO NO. 21 IN C, *K. 467*

THE FIRST MOVEMENT *Allegro maestoso* (*Quickly, with majesty*). Like one of the sublime comic characters from a Mozart-da Ponte opera, the concerto announces itself with a pungent and witty little march. It insinuates itself at the dynamic level of *piano* until it is repeated by the whole orchestra (④ 0:23), where it modulates in the most arresting manner before returning to the original key. A new subject appears, with horn calls and responses in the woodwinds (④0:51), heightening the mood. But it is not quite time for the soloist to enter: The opening march tune returns (④1:06), revealing new facets as it moves forward with implacable certainty. A contrasting softer passage is swept away by another forte statement of the march, putting the final stamp of approval on the introduction to this concerto. The orchestra, via the woodwinds (④2:04), virtually begs the soloist to enter.

The soloist's first statement is not about to challenge the swagger of the opening. It is a genteel, graceful response, borne by the chattering of the woodwinds to a level of confidence that finally brings the piano into contact with the march theme. The soloist trills over the march (④2:33), then picks up the melody alone before the orchestra returns and the piano decorates the ensemble as it moves forward. The soloist strikes out in a lovely new theme (④2:54) that begins in a dark, somewhat ambiguous manner, only to resolve itself quickly into an upbeat and cheerful mood (④4:00). For the first time the soloist sounds the melody of the march (④4:28), which the strings pick up in imitation. This response leads to a brilliant exchange that draws out the soloist (④4:46), who elaborates on and exploits this new-found boldness in the most splendid fashion. The return of the march in the orchestra, ever more assured, brings the exposition to a close, with a modulation into the key of B minor that results in a passage of remarkable beauty.

The development begins (④6:46) with a tune that ignites a series of variations. An exchange of the piano and woodwinds introduces a new subject (④7:02) that becomes a vehicle for the journey back to the original key, an experience that deepens the intensity of feeling and underscores the immense sensitivity at work here. The recapitulation arrives gently (④8:16), and Mozart achieves subtle transformations here in the variety he brings to the orchestration. A return of the march (④11:26) leads to the cadenza (in this recording, by Ferruccio Busoni) and the coda (④14:29). You may think the march will surge and end the movement with a classic "stinger." That does not happen: It simply steals away, as deftly and as wittily as it materialized in the opening bars.

THE SECOND MOVEMENT *Andante* (*Flowing*). If the slow movement of the D minor concerto wanted to carry us to Elysian fields, the C major simply wants us to dream. (This is the music used on the soundtrack of *Elvira Madigan*.) The diaphanous textures and the tender, caressing surge of the principal theme here are mesmerizing, and they seem to point toward the Romantic style (and the music of Chopin) as surely as does the drama of the D minor concerto. The movement breaks down easily into three sections. The first is orchestral, presenting the material in a luminous but straightforward manner. The second introduces the soloist (⑤1:37), who echoes the first section, with interjections from a new theme (⑤2:40) and a number of modulations that add iridescence to the melodic material. The third section (⑤5:12) sums up the first, continuing its bewitching modulations before arriving at the coda. There is little here that requires explanation—the music is of such exquisite beauty that it speaks for itself. Listen, though, to the simplicity and refinement of Mozart's orchestration—muted strings, the gentlest *pizzicati* (the plucking of the strings), and a woodwind ensemble that gleams like precious jewels.

THE THIRD MOVEMENT *Allegro vivace assai* (*Very quickly and lively*). This remarkable concerto closes with what is, comparatively speaking, a not-so-remarkable rondo. It is charming and energetic, everything such a movement should be—it simply lacks the transcendence of the two movements that precede it. After the miracle of the andante, the bubbling melody of the refrain sounds positively flippant, and it sets the tone for the entire movement. The second couplet (⑥3:57) brings on a development that offers a charming patter between the soloist and the winds, and it is followed by a return of the refrain (⑥4:24). The recapitulation offers little that is new, followed by the cadenza (6 5:52) (also by Busoni, in this recording) and a final statement of the refrain that brings the work to a close.

The Performers

Though she enjoyed relatively modest international fame, the Hungarian pianist **Annie Fischer (1914–1995)** has always been a connoisseur's favorite for her brilliant, highly cultivated approach to Mozart and Beethoven, as well as Chopin, Schumann, Liszt, Brahms, and Bartók. A student in Budapest of Erno Dohnányi, she made her debut at the age of eight, playing Beethoven's First Piano Concerto. As the youngest of 100 competitors, Fischer won first prize in Budapest's International Liszt Competition in 1933 with an inspiring performance of the massive Liszt B minor sonata. Her career was halted by World War II, but she resumed performing in its aftermath. Fischer's recordings are relatively few. She was relentlessly critical of them and unhappy with the idea of "freezing" a performance for all time, but they are prized by collectors. She ended her concert career in the summer of 1992 with a triumphant recital in London. The recordings heard here are considered among the finest of the hundreds made of these concertos.

The English conductor **Sir Adrian Boult (1899–1983)** is a legend in British music. In his student days in Leipzig, Boult heard Arthur Nikisch conduct, and he remained active in music until the dawn of the digital age. Boult conducted the orchestra for Diaghilev's Ballets Russes, taught conducting at the Royal Academy of Music, founded the BBC Symphony Orchestra during his tenure as the radio network's musical director (1930–1942), and conducted the music at the coronations of both King George VI (1937)—after which he was knighted—and Queen Elizabeth II (1953). In addition to a long and venerable international career, Boult tirelessly advocated the cause of British music. He led the Henry Wood Promenade Concerts ("the Proms") at London's Royal Albert Hall, served as musical director of the London Philharmonic Orchestra, had two stints at the helm of the City of Birmingham Symphony Orchestra, and conducted the world premieres of three of the symphonies of Ralph Vaughan Williams and Gustav Holst's *The Planets*.

The career of **Wolfgang Sawallisch (1923–)** followed the august Austro-German tradition of conducting in which a promising young musician obtains experience and seasoning in the opera house before taking on orchestral work. Sawallisch began his illustrious career as a répétiteur—a choral coach—in Germany's busy network of opera houses in 1947, steadily moving through musical director's posts with the companies in Aachen,

Wolfgang Sawallisch

Wiesbaden, and Cologne, along with a stint at the Bayreuth Festival. He also held orchestral posts with the Vienna Symphony Orchestra (1960–1970), the Hamburg State Philharmonic (1973–1981), and the Orchestre de la Suisse Romande (1970–1980). In 1971 Sawallisch became general music director of Munich's State Opera, and he assumed the position of musical director of the Philadelphia Orchestra in the 1993–94 season.

PHOTO CREDITS: Austrian Cultural Institute, New York: 3, 10, 13, 16, 18, 19, 20, 22, 23, 24, 32, 46; Sotheby's: 34; The Pierpont Morgan Library, Mary Flagler Cary Music Collection/Art Resource, NY: 17; Dover Publications, Inc.: 26, 30; The Bettmann Archive: 15, 29; EMI Records, Ltd.: Cover; EMI Records, Ltd./photo by Abe Frajndlich: 43; The British Museum: 28; Collection G.S. Fraenkel: 21.

With special thanks to the Austrian Cultural Institute, New York.